MY BROTHER, WILL

by JOAN ROBINS
illustrated by MARYLIN HAFNER

GREENWILLOW BOOKS, NEW YORK

FOR PETER, WHO ALWAYS COMES THROUGH—J. R.

FOR KAREN AND PETER—M. H.

Printed in Hong Kong
by South China Printing Co.

Library of Congress
Cataloging-in-Publication Data
Robins, Joan.
My brother, Will.
Summary:
A boy notices all of
the changes in his
baby brother, Will,
as he grows from very
young infant to independently
walking toddler.
1. Child development—
Juvenile literature.
[1. Babies.
2. Child development]
I. Hafner, Marylin, ill.
II. Title.
RJ131.R5919 1986
612'.654   85-9852
ISBN 0-688-05222-3
ISBN 0-688-05223-1 (lib. bdg.)

The illustrations are watercolor.
The text type is Quorum.

When Will came to my house
he was six days old.
He looked like this.

My mother called him Willie.
My father called him William.
But I called him Will.

When he was six months old,
Will looked like this.
He liked to sit up
with a pillow behind him.
But not for long.
Once he almost fell.
It was lucky I was keeping
my eye on him.

When Will was ten months old,
he began to crawl into everything.
I had to put all my things on the shelf.
Or in the closet—with the door shut.

"You are too much trouble, Will," I said.
"Why don't you learn to walk?"
I stood him up.
He liked it.

He stood up by himself then—
everywhere.
In his bed, in his carriage,
when we put him in the car...
But he did not walk.

Will crawled all over the beach
when he was a year old.
He liked to eat sand.
"You'll get sick, Will," I told him.
"I have to watch you every minute."

Will learned to say Mama.
He learned to say Dada.
He learned to say Kit. That's me.
(My parents call me Charles.)
And he learned to hide.

"I'll help you walk, Will," I said.
He sat down.

One day I told him I was going to school.
"You will never go to school, Will,"
I said, "if you do not learn to walk."
He grabbed my squeaky mouse.
He didn't even crawl after me to the door.

I came home from school that day
with a new friend.
"This is my brother, Will," I told Henry.
"Look how he can stand.
And he can crawl anywhere—fast.
Show Henry how you crawl, Will."

My brother can walk anywhere now—fast.
I still call him Will.
And he calls me Kit.